ANSWER TO
DR. PRIESTLEY'S LETTERS
TO A PHILOSOPHICAL UNBELIEVER

LECTOR HOUSE PUBLIC DOMAIN WORKS

ANSWER TO DR. PRIESTLEY'S LETTERS TO A PHILOSOPHICAL UNBELIEVER

MATTHEW TURNER, WILLIAM HAMMON

ISBN: 978-93-5420-021-2

Published: 1782

LECTOR HOUSE LLP
E-MAIL: lectorpublishing@gmail.com

ANSWER TO DR. PRIESTLEY'S LETTERS TO A PHILOSOPHICAL UNBELIEVER.

PART I.

BY

MATTHEW TURNER,
WILLIAM HAMMON

MDCCLXXXII

ADVERTISEMENT.

The Editor of this publication has more in object to answer Dr. Priestley than to deliver his own sentiments upon Natural Religion, which however he has no inclination to disguise: but he does not mean to be answerable for them farther, than as by reason and nature he is at present instructed. The question here handled is not so much, whether a Deity and his attributed excellences exist, as whether there is any Natural or Moral proof of his existence and of those attributes. Revealed knowledge is not descanted upon; therefore Christians at least need take no offence. Doubts upon Natural Religion have not hitherto been looked upon as attacks upon Revelation, but rather as corroborations of it. What the Editor believes as a Christian (if he is one is therefore another affair, nor does he reckon himself so infallible or incapable of alteration in his sentiments, as not at another time to adopt different ones upon more reflexion and better information; therefore, though he has at present little or no doubt of what he asserts (taken upon the principles laid down) he shall hold himself totally freed from any necessity of defending the contents of this publication if brought into controversy; and as he has no desire of making converts, hopes he shall not himself be marked out as an object of persecution.

Speculative points have always been esteemed fair matters for a free discussion. The religion established in this country is not the religion of Nature, but the religion of Moses and Jesus, with whom the writer has nothing to do. He trusts therefore he shall not be received as a malevolent disturber of such common opinions as are esteemed to keep in order a set of low wretches so inclinable to be lawless. At least, if he attempts to substitute better foundations for morality, malevolence can be no just charge. Truth is his aim; and no professors of religion will allow their system to be false. Or if he should be thought too bold a speculator, such of the ecclesiastics as will be his opponents may rather laugh at him than fear him. They have a thousand ways of making their sentiments go down with the bulk of mankind, to one this poor writer has. They are an army ready marshalled for the support of their own thesis; they are in the habit of controversy; pulpits are open to them as well as the press; and while the present author will be looked upon as a miracle of hardiness for daring to put his name to what he publishes, they can without fear or imputation lift up their heads; and should they even be known to transgress the bounds of good sense or politeness, they will only be esteemed as more zealous labourers in their own vocation.

CONTENTS

PREFATORY ADDRESS.

Dr. Priestley,

Your Letters addressed to a Philosophical Unbeliever I perused, not because I was a Philosopher or an Unbeliever; it were presumption to give myself the former title, and at that time I certainly did not deserve the latter; but as I was acquainted with another, who in reality, as far as I and others who know him can judge, deserves the title of a Philosopher and is neither ashamed nor afraid of that of an Unbeliever, I conceived them apt to be sent to my friend, and when I presented them to him, he said he was the person whom he should suppose you meant to address, if you had a particular person in view; but he had too much understanding of the world, though much abstracted from the dregs of it, not to conceive it more probable that you meant your Letters to be perused by thinking men in general, Believers and Unbelievers, to confirm the former in their creed, and to convert the latter from their error. You shall speedily know the effect they have had in both ways. For myself I must inform you that I was brought up a Believer from my infancy; a Theist, if a Christian is such; for I suppose the word will be allowed, though the equivalent term of Deist is so generally reprobated by Christians; I had before my eyes the example of a most amiable parent; a moral man, a Christian undoubtedly; who, when I have been attending upon him, as much from affection as from duty upon a sick and nearly dying bed, has prayed I might be stedfast in the faith he held, in accents still sounding in my intellectual ear; a parent, whom for his virtues and love of his offspring, like a Chinese, I am tempted to worship, and I could exclaim with the first of poets,

"Erit ille mihi semper Deus."

With such habits of education then, such fervent advice and such reverence for my instructor, what can have turned me from my belief; for I confess I am turned? Immorallity it is not; that I assert has not preceded my unbelief, and I trust never will follow it; there has not indeed yet been time for it to follow; whether it is a probable consequence will presently be discussed; but it is *thought,* free thought upon the subject; when I began freely to think I proceeded boldly to doubt; your Letters gave me the cause for thinking, and my scepticism was exchanged for conviction; not entirely by the perusal of your Letters; for I do not think they would quite have made me an Atheist! but by attention to that answer from my friend, which I have his permission to subjoin.

In mentioning that doubts arose by reading your very Letters, which were written to eradicate all doubts, let me not accuse you of being unequal to the task assumed. I mean no such charge. You have in my opinion been fully equal to the discussion, and have bandied the argument ably, pleasingly and politely. I am certain from the extracts you have made from Dr. Clarke, the first of other Divines, I should have been converted from my superstition by his reasoning, even without perusal of an answer: I pay you however the compliment of having only brought me to doubt, and I find I am not the only person who have been led to disbelieve by reading books expressly written to confirm the Believer. Stackhouse's Comment upon the Bible, and Leland's View of Deistical Writers have perhaps made as many renegado's in this country as all the allurements of Mahometanism has in others. What can be said to this? They were both undoubtedly men of abilities, and meant well to the cause they had to support. All that I shall observe upon the matter is, that what cannot bear discussion cannot be true. Reasoning in other sciences is the way to arrive at truth: the learned for a while may differ, but argument at last finds its force, and the controversy usually ends in general conviction. Reasoning upon the science of divinity will equally have its weight, and all men of letters would long ago have got rid of all superstitious notions of a Deity, but that men of letters are frequently men of weak nerves; such as Dr. Johnson is well known to be, that great triumph to religionists; it requires courage as well as sense to break the shackles of a pious education; but if merely a resolve to reason upon their force can break them, what can we observe in conclusion but

"Magnus est veritas et prevalebit."

That religion or belief of a Deity cannot bear the force of argument is well known by Divines in general, is manifest by their annexing an idea of reproach to the very term of arguing upon the subject. These arguers they call Free-thinkers, and this appellation has obtained, in the understanding of pious believers, the most odious disgrace. Yet we cannot argue without thinking; nor can we either think or argue to any purpose without freedom. Therefore free-thinking, so far from being a disgrace, is a virtue, a most commendable quality. How absurd, and how cruel it is in the professors of divinity, to address the understanding of men on the subject of their belief, and to upbraid those very men who shall exercise their understanding in attending to their arguments! No tyranny is greater than that of ecclesiastics. These chain down our very ideas, other tyrants only confine our limbs. They invite us to the argument, yet damn us to eternal punishment for the use of reason on the subject. They give to man an essence distinct from his corporeal appearance and this they call his soul, a very ray and particle of the Divine Being; the principal faculty of this soul they allow to be that of reasoning, and yet they call reason a dark lanthorn, an erroneous vapour, a false medium, and at last the very instrument of another fancied Being of their own to lead men into their own destruction. *"In the image of himself made he man."* A favourite text with theologians; but surely they do not mean that this God Almighty of theirs has got a face and person like a man. No; that they exclaim against, and, when we push them for the resemblance, they confess it is in the use of reason; it is in the soul.

I am aware that I am not here to mix questions of Christianity with the general question of a Divinity; subjects of a very distinct enquiry, and which in the Letters to a Philosophical Unbeliever are very carefully separated. The subject of revelation is indeed promised afterwards to be taken up, provided the argument in favour of Natural Religion meets with a good reception. How, Dr. Priestley, you can judge of that reception I am at a loss to know, otherwise than by the number of editions you publish. It is then in the sum total just as much as if you had said, "provided this book sells well I will write another." Yet it may be sold to many such readers as I have been, though you will hardly call such reception good. You that have wrote so much, to whom it is so easy to write more, who profess a belief of revelation, such a laborious enquirer, and so great a master of the art of reasoning, should rather have engaged at once to prove in a subsequent publication the truth of revealed religion in arguments, as candid and as fairly drawn as those you have used in proof of a Deity independent of revelation. Different as I am in qualifications from you, not very learned, far from industrious, unused to publish, I do now promise that when you shall have brought into light your intended letters in behalf of revelation I will answer them. I hope you will take it as an encouragement to write that you are sure you shall have an answer. I mean you should, and I am sure I shall think myself greatly honoured if you will descend so far as to reply to my present answer. I know you have been used in controversies to have the last word, and in this I shall not baulk your ambition; for notwithstanding any defect of my plea in favour of atheism I mean to join issue upon your replication, and by no means, according to the practice and language of the lawyers, to put in a rejoinder. Should your arguments be defectively answered by me, should your learning and your reasoning be more conspicuous than mine, I shall bear your triumph without repining.

I declare I am rather pleased there are so few atheists than at all anxious to make more. I triumph in my superior light. I am like the Jew or the Bramin who equally think themselves privileged in their superior knowledge of the Deity. With me and with my friend the comparison holds by way of contrast, for we are so proud in our singularity of being atheists that we will hardly open our lips in company, when the question is started for fear of making converts, and so lessening our own enjoyment by a numerous division of our privilege with others. It has indeed often been disputed, whether there is or ever was such a character in the world as an atheist. That it should be disputed is to me no wonder. Every thing may be, and almost every thing has been disputed. There are few or none who will venture openly to acknowledge themselves to be atheists. I know none among my acquaintance, except that one friend, to whom as a Philosophical Unbeliever I presented your Letters, and to whose answer I only mean this address as an introduction. I shall therefore not enter here into the main argument of Deity or no Deity. My address is only preliminary to the subject; but I do not therefore think myself precluded from entering into some considerations that may be thought incidental to it. I mean such considerations as whether immorality, unhappiness or timidity necessarily do or naturally ought to ensue from a system of atheism. But as to the question whether there is such an existent Being as an atheist, to put that out of all manner of doubt, I do declare upon my honour that I am one. Be it therefore for the future remembered, that in London in the kingdom of England, in the year of our Lord one thousand seven hundred and eighty-one, a man has publickly declared himself an atheist. When my friend returned me your Letters, addressing me with a grave face he said, "I hope, if you have any doubts, these

Letters will have as good effect upon you as they have had upon me." My countenance brightened up and I replied, "You are then, my friend, convinced ?" "Yes, he said, I am convinced; that is, I am most thoroughly convinced there is no such thing as a God." Behold then, if we are to be believed, two atheists instead of one.

Another question has been raised "whether a society of atheists can exist?" In other words "whether honesty sufficient for the purposes of civil society can be insured by other motives than the belief of a Deity?" Bayle has handled that question well.[1] Few who know how to reason (and it is in vain to speak or think of those who lay reason out of the case) can fail to be convinced by the arguments of Bayle. I shall discuss the question no farther than as it is necessarily included in the discussion of some of those supposed results of atheism, such as I have before mentioned in the instances of immorality, unhappiness and timidity. In my argument upon this subject I shall carefully avoid all abuse and ridicule. Controversies are apt to be acrimonious. You, Sir, have certainly shewn instances to the contrary. You have charity beyond your fellows in the ecclesiastical line, and your answerers seem not to me to have a right in fair argument to step out of the limits you have prescribed yourself. To dispute with you is a pleasure equal almost to that of agreeing with another person. You have candour enough to allow it possible that an atheist may be a moral man. Where is that other ecclesiastic who will allow the same? Your answerers ought also to hold themselves precluded from using ridicule in handling this subject. I am no great supporter of Lord Shaftesbury's doctrine that ridicule is the test of truth. I own truth can never be ridiculous, that is, it can never be worthy of laughter, but still it may be laughed at. To use the other term, I may say, truth can never be worthy of ridicule, but still it may be ridiculed. Just ridicule is a sufficient test of truth; but after all we should be driven to an inquiry, upon the principles of reasoning, whether the ridicule were just or not. Boldness, which is not incompatible with decency and candour, I do hold to be an absolute requisite in all speech and argument, where truth is the object of inquiry. Therefore when I am asked, whether there is a God or no God, I do not mince the matter, but I boldly answer there is none, and give my reason for my disbelief; for I adopt my friend's answer by the publication of it.

That mischief may ensue to society by such freedom of discussion is also another argument for me to consider; I do not say to combat, for though I were convinced or could not resist the argument that mischief would ensue to society by such a discussion, yet I should think myself intitled to enter into it. I have a right to truth, and to publish truth, let society suffer or not suffer by it. That society which suffers by truth should be otherwise constituted; and as I cannot well think that truth will hurt any society rightly constituted, so I should rather be inclined to doubt the force of the argument in case atheism being found to be truth should apparently be proved prejudicial to such a society.

I come unprejudiced to the question, and when I have promised you an answer to your future Letters in support of revelation, I have neither anticipated your argument nor prejudged the cause. I hold myself open to be convinced, and if I am convinced I shall say so, which is equally answering as if I denied the force

---

[1] *Pensees sur la Comete.*

of your observations. In that sense only I promise an answer. If I believe I shall say, I do; but I shall not believe and tremble, confident as I am, that if I act an honest part in life, whether there be a Deity and a future existence or not, whatever reason I may have to rejoice in case such ideas he realised, I can upon such an issue have none to tremble. I look upon myself to have more reason to be temporally afraid than eternally so. Dr. Priestley or any other Doctor can put his name boldly to a book in favour of Theism, loudly call the supporters of a contrary doctrine to the argument, and if no answer is produced, assert their own reasoning to be unanswerable. In that sense their sort of reasoning has been frequently unanswerable. Here however is an instance of a poor unknown individual, making experience of the candour of the ecclesiastics and the equity of the laws of England, for he ventures to subscribe his publication with his name as well as Dr. Priestley does his Letters, to which this publication is an answer. Perhaps he may have cause to repent of his hardiness, but if he has, he is equally resolved to glory in his martyrdom, as to suffer it. Whatever advantage religion has had in the enumeration of it's martyrs, the cause of atheism may boast the same. As to the instances of the professors of any particular form of religion, or modification of that form, such as Christians or sects of Christians, suffering martyrdom for their belief, I shall no more allow them to be martyrs for theism than Pagans similarly suffering for their belief, shall I call martyrs for atheism. Theism very likely has had it's martyrs. I can instance one I think in Socrates, and I shall mention Vanini as a martyr for atheism. The conduct of those two great men in their last moments may be worth attending to. The variety of other poor heretical wretches, who have been immolated at the shrine of absurdity for all the possible errors of human credence, let them have their legendary fame. I put them out of the scale in this important inquiry.

Not that I really think the argument to be much advanced by naming the great supporters of one opinion or of another. In mathematics, mechanics, natural philosophy, in literature, taste, and politics the sentiments of great men of great genius are certainly of weight. There are some subjects capable of demonstration, many indeed which the ingenuity of one man can go farther to illustrate than that of another. The force of high authority is greater in the three former sciences than in the latter. Theism and Atheism I hold to be neither of them strictly demonstrable. You, Dr. Priestley, agree with me in that. Still I hold the question capable of being illustrated by argument, and I should hold the authority of great men's names to be of more weight in this subject, were I not necessarily forced to consider that all education is strongly calculated to support the idea of a Deity; by this education prejudice is introduced, and prejudice is nothing else than a corruption of the understanding. Certain principles, call them, if you please, data, must be agreed upon before any reasoning can take place. Disputants must at least agree in the ideas which they annex to the language they use. But when prejudice has made a stand, argumentation is set at so wide a distance, through a want of fixt data to proceed upon, that attention is in vain applied to the dispute. Besides, the nature of the subject upon which this prejudice takes place, is such, that the finest genius is nearly equally liable to an undue bias with the most vulgar. To question with boldness and indifference, whether an individual, all-forming, all-seeing and all-governing Being exists, to whom, if he exists, we may possibly be responsible for our actions, whose intelligence and power must be infinitely superior to our own, requires a great conquest of former habitude, a firmness of nerves, as well as of understanding; it will therefore be no great wonder, if such men as Locke and Newton can be named among the believers in a Deity. They were christians as well as theists, so that their authority goes as far in one respect as in the other. But if the opinions of men of great genius are to have weight, what is to be said of modern men of genius? You, Sir, are of opinion that the world is getting wiser as well as better. There is all the reason in the world it should get wiser at least, since wisdom is only a collection of experience, and there must be more experience as the world is older. Modern Philosophers are nearly all atheists. I take the term atheist here in the popular sense. Hume, Helvetius, Diderot, D'Alembert. Can they not weigh against Locke and Newton, and even more than Locke and Newton, since their store of knowledge and learning was at hand to be added to their own, and among them are those who singly possessed equal science in mathematics as in meta-physics? It is not impossible, perhaps not improbable, from his course of learning and inquiries, that if Dr. Priestley had not from his first initiation into science been dedicated for what is called the immediate service of God, he himself might have been one of the greatest disprovers of his pretended divinity.

In England you think, Sir, that atheism is not prevalent among men of free reasoning, though you acknowledge it to be much so in other countries. It is not the first time it has been observed that the greater the superstition of the common people the less is that of men of letters. In the heart of the Papal territories perhaps is the greatest number of atheists, and in the reformed countries the greatest number of deists. Yet it is a common observation, especially by divines, that deism leads to atheism, and I believe the observation is well founded. I hardly need explain here, that by deism in this sense is meant a belief in the existence of a Deity from natural and philosophical principles, and a disbelief in all immediate revelation by the Deity of his own existence. Such is the force of habit, that it is by degrees only, that even men of sense and firmness shake off one prejudice after another. They begin by getting rid of the absurdities of all popular religions. This leaves them simple deists, but the force of reasoning next carries them a step farther, and whoever trusts to this reasoning, devoid of all fear and prejudice, is very likely to end at last in being an atheist. Nor do I admit it to be an argument either for Revelation or Natural Religion, that the same turn for speculation that would convert a christian into a theist, will carry him on to be an atheist, though I know the argument has been often used. If upon sick beds or in dying moments men revert to their old weakness and superstitions, their falling off may afford triumph to religionists; for my part I care not so much for the opinions of sick and dying men, as of those who at the time are strong and healthy. But in the opinion of the one or the other I put no great stress. My faith is in reasoning, for though ridicule is not a complete test of truth, reasoning I hold certainly to be so. I own belief may be imprest on the mind otherwise than by the force of reason. The mind may be diseased. All I shall say is that though I have formerly believed many things without reason, and even many against it, as is very common, I hope I shall never more. My mind (I was going to say, thank God) is sane at present, and I intend to keep it so. I am aware that at the expression just used some will exclaim in triumph, that the poor wretch could not help thinking of his God at the same time he was denying him. The observation would hold good, if it were not that we often speak and write unpremeditately and though what is in this manner unpremeditately expressed upon a revision should be certainly expunged, yet I chuse to leave the expression to shew the force of habit.

In fear lies the origin of all fancied deities, whether sole or numberless.

Primus in orbe Deos fecit Timor.

But the great debasement of the human mind is evidenced in the instance of attributing a merit to belief, which has come at last to be stiled a virtue, and is dignified by the name of faith, that most pitiful of all human qualities. When the apostle spoke of faith, hope and charity, he might as well have exclaimed the least of the three is faith, as the greatest is charity.

One enthusiast cries out *un Roi* and another *un Dieu*. The reality of the king I admit, because I feel his power. Against my feeling and my experience I cannot argue, for upon these sensations is built all argument. But not all the wondrous works of the creation, as I hear the visible operations of nature called, convince me in the least of the existence of a Deity. By nature I mean to express the whole of what I see and feel, that whole, I call self-existent from all eternity; I admit a principle of intelligence and design, but I deny that principle to be extraneous from itself. My creed in fine is the same with that of the Roman poet;

"Deus est ubicunque movemur."

If then I am admitted to explain my deity in this sense, I am not an atheist, nor can any one else in the world be such. The *vis naturae*, the perpetual industry, intelligence and provision of nature must be apparent to all who see, feel or think. I mean to distinguish this active, intelligent and designing principle, inherent as much in matter as the properties of gravity or any elastic, attractive or repulsive power, from any extraneous foreign force and design in an invisible agent, supreme though hidden lord and maker over all effects and appearances that present themselves to us in the course of nature. The last supposition makes the universe and all other organised matter a machine made or contrived by the arbitrary will of another Being, which other Being is called God; and my theory makes a God of this universe, or admits no other God or designing principle than matter itself and its various organisations.

The inquiry is said to be important. But why is it so! All truth is important. It is a question of little importance, merely whether a man had a maker or no, although it is of great importance to disprove the existence of such a Deity as theologians wish to establish, because appearances in the world go against it. Supposing however that it was granted, that the question, whether there is a Deity or not, was as little important as other truths, yet the question becomes important with this reflexion, that other events may follow as deductions; such as a particular providence, or a future state of rewards and punishments; but whether such deductions or either of them necessarily follow may well be queried. As to a particular providence you give up the reality of it, and I give it up too. But I cannot give up the argument, that if there were a God with all his allowed attributes of wisdom, power and justice, there ought to be a particular providence to counteract the general laws of nature, in favour of those who defend the interposition. Though the Deity should not interfere unless there be a worthy cause, agreeable to the Horation rule,

"Nec Deus interfuit nisi vindice nodus;"

Yet surely from the same principles it should follow that the Deity ought to interfere where there is a worthy cause. Here however arises another dilemma, for if the Deity has really those attributes of power and justice, there would never have been occasion for such temperaneous interpositions. A particular providence must indeed prove one of these two principles, either that God was imperfect in his design, or that inert matter is inimical to the properties of God. If that wished for interposition of the Deity is put off to a future existence, I cannot help observing, that future day has been already a long while waited for in vain, and any delay destroys some one attribute or other of the Deity. He wants justice, or he wants the power, or the will to do good and be just. That a future state of rewards and punishments may however exist without a Deity, you, Dr. Priestley, allow to be no impossibility. It may indeed be argued with apparent justness, that a principle of reviviscence may as well be admitted as a principle of production in the first instance: and as to rewards and punishments, judgement may be rendered, as well as now, by Beings less than Deities. For my part I firmly wish for such a future state, and though I cannot firmly believe it, I am resolved to live as if such a state were to ensue. This seems, I own, like doubting, and doubting may be said to be a miserable state of anxiety. "Better be confident than unhinged; better confide in ignorance than have no fixed system." So it may be argued; but I think the result will be as people feel. Those who do not feel bold enough, to be satisfied with their own thoughts, may abandon them and adopt the thoughts of others. For my part I am content with my own; and not the less so because they do not end in certainty upon matters, from the nature of them, beyond the complete reach of human intelligence.

There is nothing in fact important to human nature but happiness, which is or ought to be the end or aim of our being. I mean self-happiness; but fortunately for mankind, such is by nature our construction, that we cannot individually be happy unless we join also in promoting the happiness of others. Should immorality, timidity or other base principles arise from atheism it tends immediately, I will own, to the unhappiness of mankind. If it is asked me, "why am I honest and honourable?" I answer, because of the satisfaction I have in being so. "Do all people receive that satisfaction?" No, many who are ill educated, ill-exampled and perverted, do not. I do, that is enough for me. In short, I am well constructed, and I feel I can therefore act an honest and honourable part without any religious motive. Did I perceive, that belief in a Deity produced morality or inspired courage, I might be prompted to confess, that the contrary would ensue from atheism. But the bulk of the world has long believed, or long pretended to believe in a Deity, yet morality and every commendable quality seem at a stand. The believer and the unbeliever we often see equally base, equally immoral. Superstition is certainly only the excess of religion. That evidently is attended often with immorality and cowardice. I am tempted to say, from observation, that the belief of a Deity is apt to drive mankind into vice and baseness; but I check myself in the assertion, upon considering that very few indeed are those who really believe in a Deity out of such as pretend to do so. It is impossible for an intellectual being to believe firmly in that of which he can give no account, or of which he can form no conception. I hold the Deity, the fancied Deity, at least, of whom with all his attributes such pompous descriptions are set forth to the great terror of old women and the amusement of young children, to be an object of which we form (as appears when we scrutinise into our ideas) no conception and therefore can give no account. It is said, after all this, that men do still believe in such a Deity, I then do say in return, they do not make use of their intellects. The moment we go into a belief beyond what we feel, see and understand, we might as well believe in will-with-a-whisp as in God. But I would fix morality upon a better basis than belief in a Deity. If it has indeed at present no other basis, it is not morality, it is selfishness, it is timidity; it is the hope of reward, it is the dread of punishment. For a great and good man, shew me one who loves virtue because he finds a pleasure in it, who has acquired a taste for that pleasure by considering what and where happiness is, who is not such a fool as to seek misery in preference to happiness, whose honour is his Deity, whose conscience is his judge. Put such a man in combat against the superstitious son of Spain or Portugal, it were easy to say who would shew the truest courage. The question might be more voluminously discussed, but I feel already proof of conviction; if you, Dr. Priestley, do not, perhaps some other readers may. I have nothing to do with men of low minds. They will always have their religion or pretence of it, but I am mistaken if it is not the gallows or the pillory that more govern their morals than the gospel or the pulpit.

After all, atheism may be a system only for the learned. The ignorant of all ages have believed in God. The answer of a Philosophical Unbeliever though written in the vulgar tongue may probably not reach the vulgar. If argument had prevailed they were long converted from their superstitious belief. The sentiments of atheistical philosophers have long been published. If mischief therefore could ensue to society from such free discussions, that mischief society must long have felt. I think truth should never be hid, but few are those who mind it. I will therefore take upon myself but little importance though I have presumed to preface an answer from a Philosophical Unbeliever to Letters which you, Dr. Priestley have written. If you deem that answer detrimental to the interests of society, you will recollect that you invite the proposal of objections and promise to answer all as well as you can. If you should happen to be exasperated by the freedom of the language or the contrariety of the sentiment, this answer will gain weight in proportion as you lose in the credit of a tolerant Divine. Therefore if you reply at all, reply with candour and with coolness; heed the matter and not the man, though I subscribe my name, and am

Reverend Sir,
Your friend, admirer, and humble servant,
WILLIAM HAMMON.

Oxford-Street, No. 418. Jan. 1, 1782.

ANSWER FROM A
PHILOSOPHICAL UNBELIEVER.

It is the general fashion to believe in a God, the maker of all things, or at least to pretend to such a belief, to define the nature of this existing Deity by the attributes which are given to him, to place the foundation of morality on this belief, and in idea at least, to connect the welfare of civil society with the acknowledgement of such a Being. Few however are those, who being questioned can give any tolerable grounds for their assertions upon this subject, and hardly any two among the learned agree in their manner of proving what each will separately hold to be indisputably clear. The attributes of a Deity are more generally agreed upon, though less the subject of proof, than his existence. As to morality, those very people who are moral will not deny, they would be so though there were not a God, and there never yet has been a civil lawgiver, who left crimes to be punished by the author of the universe; not even the profanation of oaths upon the sacredness of which so much is built in society, and which yet is said to be a more immediate offence against the Deity than any other that can be named.

The method which Dr. Priestley has taken to prove the existence of a God, is by arguing from *effect* to *cause*. He explodes that other pretended proof *a priori* which has so much raised the fame of Dr. Clarke among other theologians. As to the attributes of the Deity, Dr. Priestley is not quite so confident in his proofs there; and the most amiable one, the most by mortals to be wished for, the *benevolence* of God he almost gives up, or owns at least there is not so much proof of it as of his other attributes. His observations are divided into several Letters, this is one answer given to the whole; for it would be to no purpose to reply to topics upon which the writers are agreed. What therefore is not contradicted here, Dr. Priestley may in general take to be allowed; but to obviate doubts and to allow his argument every force, it may be fairer perhaps to recite at full length what in this answer is allowed to be true, what is denied as false, what meant to be exposed as absurd, and what rejected as assertions without proof, inadmissible or inconclusive. The conclusion will contain some observations upon the whole.

TRUISMS.

1. "Effects have their adequate causes."

2. "Nothing begins to exist without a cause foreign to itself."

3. "No being could make himself, for that would imply that he existed and did not exist at the same time."

4. If one horse, or one tree, had a cause, all had."

5. Something must have existed from all eternity.

6. "Atoms cannot be arranged, in a manner expressive of the most exquisite design, without competent intelligence having existed somewhere."

7. "The idea of a supreme author is more pleasing to a virtuous mind, than that of a blind fate and fatherless deserted world."

8. "The condition of mankind is in a state of melioration, as far as misery arises from ignorance, for as the world grows older it must grow wiser, if wisdom arises from experience."

9. "All moral virtue is only a modification of benevolence."

10. "Virtue gives a better chance for happiness than vice."

11. "No instance of any revival."

12. "Atheists are not to think themselves quite secure with respect to a future life."

13. "Thought might as well depend upon the construction of the brain, as upon any invisible substance extraneous to the brain."

14. "If the works of God had a beginning, there must have been a time when he was inactive."

15. "Where happiness is wanting in the creation I would rather conclude the author had mist of his design than that he wanted benevolence."

FALSE ASSERTIONS.

1. "A cause needs not be prior to an effect."

2. "If the species of man had no beginning, it would not follow that it had no cause."

3. "A cause may be cotemporary with the effect."

4. "An atheist must believe he was introduced into the world without design."

ABSURDITIES.

1. "A general mass of sensation consisting of various elements borrowed from the past and the future."

2. "Since sensation is made up of past, present, and future, the infant feeling for the moment only, the man recollecting what is past and anticipating the future, and as the present sensation must therefore in time bear a less proportion to the general mass of sensation than it did, so at last all temporary affections, whether of pain or pleasure become wholly inconsiderable."

3. "The great book of nature and the book of revelation both lie open before us."

4. "A conclusion above our comprehension."

5. "A whole eternity already past."

6. "Since a finite Being cannot be infinitely happy, because he must then be infinite in knowledge and power; and as all limitation of happiness must consist in degree of happiness or mixture of misery, the Deity can alone determine which mode of limitation is best."

7. "We have reason to be thankful for our pains and distress."

8. "If the divine Being had made man at first as happy as he can be after all the feelings and ideas of a painful and laborious life, it must have been in violation of all general laws and by a constant and momentary interference of the Deity."

9. "It is better the divine agency should not be very conspicuous."

10. "If good prevails on the whole, creation being infinite, happiness must be infinite, and God comprehending the whole, will only perceive the balance of good, and that will be happiness unmixed with misery."

11. "If a man is happy in the whole he is infinitely happy in the whole of his existence."

12. "Although all things fall alike to all men and no distinction is made between the righteous and the wicked, and even though the wicked derive an advantage from their vices, yet this is consistent with a state of moral government by a Being of infinite wisdom and power."

13. "As ploughing is the means of having a harvest, though God has predetermined whether there should be a harvest or not, so prayer is the means of obtaining good from God, although that good is predetermined upon; it is therefore no more absurd to pray than to plough."

14. "Notwithstanding happiness is the necessary consequence of health, yet man's happiness is more from intellectual than corporeal feelings."

15. "Evil is necessarily connected with and subservient to good, although in the next world there will be all good and no evil."

16. "By reason we can discover the necessary existence of a Deity, yet to be a sceptic on that subject is the first step to be a Christian, because reason not sufficiently proving it we fly to revealed truth."

17. "The power, which a man has by the comprehensiveness of his mind to enjoy the future, has no apparent limits."

18. "It is of no avail in the argument concerning the existence of a Deity, that we have no conception of him, since it does not imply impossibility of his existence that we have no idea at all upon the subject."

INADMISSIBLE OR INCONCLUSIVE.

1. "The question of the existence of a Deity is important."

2. "A Theist has a higher sense of personal dignity than an atheist."

3. "The conduct of an atheist must give concern to those who are not so."

4. "An atheist believes himself to be, at his death, for ever excluded from returning life."

5. "There are more atheists than unbelievers in revelation."

6. "Men of letters may have the same bias to incredulity as others to credulity, because they are subject to a wrong association of ideas, as well as other persons though in a less degree."

7. "Whoever first made a thing, for example a chair or a table, must have had an adequate idea of it's nature and use."

8. "If a table had a designing cause, the tree from whence the wood came, and the man who made the table must have had a designing cause, which comprehended all the powers and properties of trees and men."

9. "All the visible universe, as far as we can judge, bears the marks of being one work, and therefore must have had a cause of infinite power and intelligence."

10. "We might as well say a table had no cause, as that the world had none."

11. "A Being originally and necessarily capable of comprehending itself, it is not improper to call infinite, for we can have no idea of any bounds to it's knowledge or power."

12. "A series of finite causes cannot possibly be carried back *ad infinitum*."

13. "Our imagination revolts at the idea of an intellectual soul of the universe, that is, of an intelligence resulting from arrangement."

14. "The actual existence of the universe compels us to come at last to an *originally existent and intellectual Being*, because if the immediate maker of the universe has not existed from all eternity, he must have derived his being and senses from one who has, and that being we call God."

15. "God must be present to all his works, if we admit no power can act but where it is, he must therefore exist every where, because his works are every where."

16. "As no being can unmake or materially change himself (at least none can annihilate himself) so God is unchangeable, for no Being God made can change him and no other Being can exist but what God made."

17. "Two infinite intelligent beings of the same kind would coincide, therefore there can only be one God."

18. "Nothing can be more evident, than that plants and animals could not have proceeded from each other from all eternity."

19. "That happiness is the design of the creation because health is designed and sickness is only an exception, not a general rule is as evident as that the design of the Mill-wright must have been, that his machine should not be obstructed."

20. "As a state of sickness is comparatively rare with a state of health, happiness the result of health, and the end of the creation happiness, so the end of the creation is already in a great measure answered."

21. "Pleasure tends to continue and propagate itself, pain to check and exterminate itself."

22. "As our knowledge and power in respect to shunning pains and procuring pleasures advance with our experience, nothing is wanting to enable us to exterminate all pains, but a continuance of being.

23. "Our enjoyments continually increase in real value from infancy to old age."

24. "A future moral distribution is probable, because God is infinitely powerful and wise."

25. "Since reverence, gratitude, obedience, confidence are duties to men, so they are to God; and as we pray to men, so we should pray to God."

26. "Prescience, predetermination and infinite benevolence are no argument against prayer to the Deity."

27. "A wish produced by nature is evidence of the thing wished for, but a future state is wished for, therefore there is evidence of a future state."

28. "As we have no idea how we came originally to be produced, for what we know to the contrary our reproduction may be as much the course of nature as our original production.."

29. "A gloom and melancholy belong more to atheists than to devout people."

OBSERVATIONS.

Dr. Priestley will hardly doubt, after this collection from his work that it has at least been read before it is attempted to be answered. It is in the writer's power to quote the page and line for each assertion, but it would be stuffing this publication with unnecessary references. Dr. Priestley will be able to know what are his own sentiments and what not without recurring to his printed Letters. There has been also another difficulty in classing the several exceptions under the different heads; what is false, what is absurd, and what is inadmissible bordering so nearly on each other. Nice distinctions cannot in such respect be made, but the whole together form the main argument which is to be answered.

The first and principal assertion is, that effects have their adequate cause; it is then added, that the universe is an effect, that it therefore must have a cause, and to this cause in the English language is given the name of God. This proposition is true, provided the universe is an effect, but that is a *postulatum* without concession and without a proof. This *original Being* he advances in another place to be that only something which existed uncaused from all eternity, and which could not have been a Being, like a man or a table, incapable of comprehending, itself, for such existences would require another superior Being. But if the universe is not adopted as an effect, if it is taken as existing from all eternity, the universe becomes an intelligent Being, and there or no where is the Deity sought after. Such a Being we may properly speak of and reason upon. The whole is subjected to our sensations and our experience. But of his own *uncaused Being* Dr. P. says we cannot properly speak. Is not that alone an argument of there being no such thing? His friend Dr. Clarke says, we cannot have an idea of an impossible thing. Now this discovered Deity is allowed to be that of which we can have no idea. So far at least it is allied to the impossible.

As to the argument of cause and effect, the latter certainly implies the former; but when we give the name of effect to any thing, we must be certain it is an effect, for we may be so far mistaken perhaps as to call that an effect which is a cause, at least what is an effect to-day may be a cause to-morrow, as in the instance of generation; for though a son does not beget his father, he too has his offspring in which he may be said to live over again, and if we are to argue only from experience, most probably that alone is the resurrection and the life to come. But if it is contended that our experience relates only to finite causes, or causes incapable of comprehending themselves, it must at the same time be allowed, that all our reasoning is founded only on experience. This Dr. P. at least allows even while he keeps reasoning about a Deity, which he calls an infinite cause capable of comprehending itself, though nobody is capable of comprehending it, and of which we therefore can have no experience. Yet he will assert, that *thinking* persons seldom are convinced by *thinking*. This is odd language for a reasoner. When another philosopher or divine attempts to prove a God in their own way, Dr. Priestley can readily see his fallacies and absurdities. Dr. Clarke, the former great champion of God Almighty, is made very light of. He thought, foolish man, to prove the existence of a Deity merely by our having an idea of that existence, which would go to prove the truth of every unnatural conceit that ever entered into the heart of man; and contended farther that it would be equally absurd to suppose no Deity as two and two did not make four. It would indeed be absurd, says Dr. Priestley provided we agreed that the universe is a *caused* existence, for God is the name we give for the cause of the universe, which in such case must exist. It is only denying that the universe is a caused existence, and then the absurdity is taken away. Dr. Priestley, for the sake of making Dr. Clarke absurd, will readily allow the denial capable of being made; and for the same purpose he seems gravely to have taken upon himself to prove that school-boy's difficulty, that two and two do make four, for he says, that four is the term agreed upon in language to be given to the sum total of two and two, and that to deny the Deity is at least not so absurd as to say that two and two do not make four.

Dr. Priestley says he finds no difficulty in excluding every thing from the mind except space and duration. He allows then at least, that there is no manifest absurdity in supposing there is no Deity, for nothing can be proved by reasoning if the conclusion can be denied without absurdity, nor can there be a manifest absurdity in denying the existence of what there is no difficulty in excluding from the mind. Yet after all he adds (somewhat inconsistently) that we cannot exclude the idea of a Deity, if we do not exclude an existent universe. This Deity he defines to be a most simple Being; simple and infinite; terms which but ill agree together.

The infinite or boundless existence of this pretended Deity is a property more insisted upon than any other, and whatever other properties are given to him they are all in the infinite degree. The properties alledged to be proved are, eternity, infinite knowledge and power, unchangeableness, unity, omnipotence, action from all eternity, and independence. Benevolence and moral government are also ascribed to him but confessedly with a less degree of certainty, though the most desireable of all his given properties. Upon the subject of benevolence, Dr. Priestley only advances, that where it is not proved by the happiness of his creatures to exist, he would rather chuse to conclude he mist of his design, that is, he wanted power or knowledge, than that he wanted benevolence. If he means to argue that it is more rational to conclude this Deity wanted power and knowledge than that he wanted benevolence, and because Dr. Priestley fancies himself to have proved the Deity cannot want the two former, he concludes the Deity cannot want the latter, as the less probable for him to be deficient in, his argument is no more a truism. As a wish, that the Deity may not want benevolence, in that sense let him take it as agreed upon. He allows that misery in the human species proves malevolence in the Deity, and happiness the contrary. All the proof adduced in favour of benevolence is in asserting that throughout the universe, good is more predominant than evil. The infinite extent of benevolence he will allow incapable of proof; but then it is said that the evils which mankind endure are not so great as might be inflicted upon them; that virtue to vice, happiness to misery, health to sickness bear at least equal proportions. That lesser evils exist instead of greater is indeed but a poor proof in the favour of the benevolence of an all-powerful Being. Or grant, that good is more predominant than evil, this surely is no proof neither of the benevolence of a kind and all-powerful Being. Yet Dr. Priestley adds that the general benevolence of the Deity is unquestionable. How unquestionable? It is questioned by the author himself, and he declares he cannot prove it. After this he asks, who will pretend to dictate to such a Being? He might in the same stile conclude that no objection deserved a reply. The whole of this is absurd; but when the Doctor begins to feel enthusiasm he is like the rest of the ecclesiastical arguers. They reason themselves into imaginary Beings with more imaginary properties and then fall down and worship them. God is said to have made man in the image of himself. If he has done so, man is up with him, for he in return makes God in his own image. Much as the imagination of one man differs from another, so differs the God of each devotee. They are all idolaters or anthropomorphites to a man; there is none but an atheist that is not the one or the other.

The admission of evil into the world is an argument so exceedingly conclusive against at least a good Deity, that it is curious to see how Dr. Priestley studies to get rid of that difficulty. He partly denies the fact, at least he says there is more good than evil in the world. At last he even turns evil into good, or what ought to be the effects of one, into what ought to be the effects of the other, as he says pain is necessary for happiness. But if pain is, as he says, in this world necessary for happiness, why will it not still be necessary hereafter? He answers, because by that time we shall have experienced pain enough for a future supply of happiness. If it is objected, why have we not had pain enough by the time each of us are twenty or thirty years of age, instead of waiting 'till our deaths at so many different ages? He can only finish his argument by allowing that the ways of God are inscrutable to man, that every thing is for the best and refer us to *Candide* for the rest of his philosophy; nor will he ever resolve the question, "if evil and pain are good and necessary now, why will they not always be so? Take a view of human existence, and who can even allow, that there is more happiness than misery in the world? Dr. Priestley thinks to give the turn of the scale to happiness, by making it depend intirely upon health, notwithstanding he says in another place that human sensations are a mass collected from the past, present and future, and as a man grows up the present goes on to bear a less proportion to the other two. It would indeed be a short but lame way of proving that "happiness is the design of the creation" because health is designed, and sickness is only an exception, not a general rule." Many a healthy man has certainly been unhappy, or else had a man better study health than virtue. If the mill-wright make a poor machine he is a poor workman; God in like manner designing health and introducing sickness is but a poor physician. In another place Dr. Priestley having considered, that he had asserted that human sensations arise from ideas of the past and future as well as the present, finds himself obliged to alter his notions of happiness, so far as to say that happiness is more intellectual than corporeal. But it is rather extraordinary to assert at the same time, that happiness is the necessary consequence of health, and that happiness is more from intellectual than corporeal feelings. Surely health, if any thing, is corporeal. Another curious fancy about pain and happiness is, that our finite nature not admitting infinite or unlimited happiness we must leave it to the wisdom of the Deity to determine which is best for us (since happiness must be diminished) a little pain to be added to it or somewhat of happiness to be taken away. It hardly requires the skill of a benevolent Deity to determine which is best for the creatures he has made (and whom he wishes to be as happy as their finite nature will admit) to lessen their degree of happiness or mix therein a proportion of misery. To conclude he asks, "how it is possible to teach children caution, but by feeling pain?" It is easy to allow in answer, that it might not perhaps be possible in us. But he is arguing about the benevolence of a Deity. It was possible, he will allow, in him to have given these children knowledge without pain, at least if he continues to him the attribute he allows of omnipotence.

Next he observes that parents suspend at times their benefits to their off-spring, when persuaded they are not for their good; so does the Deity. But before this argument holds he must therefore say, it is not for the good of man to be made happy now, and that the Deity can be infinitely benevolent without willing either infinite or universal happiness. Take the argument any way, it must go against his benevolence or his power; and the same observations hold as to his love of justice, whilst he is so tardy in punishing offenders.

After observing that things are in an improving state, Dr. Priestley allows, that the moral government of the universe is not perfect. From thence he proceeds to assert, that atheists may believe it within the course of nature, that men as moral agents may after death be re-produced, and therefore that there may be a future state though there be no God, because he reasons it may be in the course of nature. This allows that the course of nature may be as it is without a God, and that there is therefore no *natural* proof of a Deity. His farther argument on this head is, that "things usually happen in a state of nature that are proper. A future state is proper. (To carry on the supposed state of melioration and complete the moral govern-ment of the universe.) It is therefore probable." This is an argument perhaps more of wish than probability, but let it have such force as belongs to it. It is not the wish of the answerer by supporting atheism to give encouragement to immorality, but should he unwarily or with weak minds do so, the argument of the Deity's exis-tence is independent of such considerations. It were better to seek another support for morality than a belief in God; for the moral purpose in believing a Deity (an invisible Being, maker of all, our moral governor, who will hereafter take cog-nizance of our conduct,) is not a little checked by considering, that he leaves the proof of his very existence so ambiguous, that even men with a habit of piety upon them cannot but have their doubts, whilst on this existence so much of the moral purpose depends. If this is not an argument against the morality of a Deity, it is at all events one against his *infinite* morality though moral is an attribute to be given to him in the infinite degree as much as any other.

It is said, infinite intelligence must have procured a necessary fitness of things, and that this forms morality. "His will could not be biassed by other influence; therefore he must have willed morality, because necessarily fit. Then comes infinite power, and yet no morality in the world or a very small portion of it. We cannot to any purpose, do what we will, argue against experience. That it must be, yet that it is not. What must be, will be. If it is not, there is no *must* in the case.

It is next said, that virtue gives a better chance for happiness than vice. This also is but a weak argument for the moral government of the universe, unless it be for a moral government by chance. Virtue ought to be the certain and immediate parent of happiness, if a moral governor existed with an uncontrouled dominion. If virtue tends to happiness, or has only a better chance of doing so, it is allowed, that a sensible atheist should hold it right to be virtuous. The latter end of a righteous man is certainly more likely to be happy than that of an unrighteous one. But let an atheist be righteous, and he can be as certain of happiness in his latter end as any other. Let another life be desirable, as it certainly is, his doubts upon it will not prevent it. Who could wish an end better or more happy than that of Mr. Hume, who most indubitably was an atheist. But if an atheist be not so good as a Theist, Dr. Priestley perhaps, will allow him to be better than a sceptic, as any principles for systematising nature are better than none at all. A Theist is not without his doubts as well as the sceptic; an atheist, once firmly becoming so, will never doubt more; for we may venture to say no miracles or new appearances will present themselves to him to draw his belief aside.

Still every thing is as God intended it—so asserts Dr. Priestley; and therefore it cannot by him be denied that crimes and vices, are of his intention. The Theist exclaims in triumph, "He that made the eye, must he not see?" But who made the eye? Or grant that God made the eye, which can only see in the light, must he necessarily see in the dark? It is again asserted, "the power which formed an eye had something in view as certainly as he that constructed a telescope. If any Being formed any eye, grant it. But if the eye exists necessarily as a part of nature; as much as any other matter, or combination of matter, necessarily existed, the result of the argument is intirely different.

It is far from being a necessary part of the atheist's creed to exclude design from the universe. He places that design in the energy of nature, which Dr. Priestley gives to some other extraneous Being. It is rather inconsistent also in him to say, that an atheist rightly judging of his own situation upon his own principles, ought not to hold himself quite secure from a future state of responsibility and existences, and yet to say he must in his own ideas hold himself soon to be excluded for ever from life.

As to the immutability of the Deity, it is difficult to guess how that is proved, except by the argument of *Lucus a non lucendo*, because every thing is changing here; therefore the Deity never changes; which is neither an argument *a priori* nor *posteriore*, but *sui generis*, merely applicable to the Deity.

From the imperial infinite intelligence of the Deity an argument is formed of his unity. Dr. Priestley says, "that two *infinite* intelligent Beings would coincide, and therefore that there can only be one such Being." Two parallels will never coincide. That is one of the first axioms of Euclid, in whom Dr. Priestley believes as much as in his bible. If the Beings are infinite in extent and magnitude they must certainly coincide, but if they are only infinite in intelligence, it does not seem to be necessary that they should.

The ubiquity of God is proved in this short way: "God made every thing, God controuls every thing. No power can act but where it is. Therefore God is present every where. The workman must certainly be present at his work, but when the work is done he may go about other business. If all the properties of matter, such as gravity, elasticity and other such existed only by the perpetual leave and agency of the Deity, it may be argued he is in all places where matter is. Space, empty space will still exist without him. In this mode of proof Dr. Priestley must, contrary to the Newtonian system argue for a *Plenum*, before he proves the ubiquity. He cannot exclude space from his mind, nor can he exclude gravity from matter. Yet can he admit matter as well as space to be eternal, because he will not allow the inactivity of God." "If God's works had a beginning he must have been *for a whole eternity* inactive." He seems to have an odd notion of eternity, for he there allows it could have an end. The argument would be fairer in concluding "he must have been inactive *or doing something else.*"

The Deity set up, if not the creator of matter, is at least the matter of it, nor will his advocates by any means allow him to be material himself. They see some incongruity in admitting one piece of matter to be so complete a master of another. However Dr. Priestley and other arguers for a Deity would do well to consider, that whatever is not matter, is a space that matter may occupy. Therefore if God is not matter, and also is not space, he is nothing. Dr. Priestley allows matter eternal, and its properties of gravity, elasticity, electricity and others equally eternal. He says directly, that matter cannot exist without it's perpetually corresponding powers. The adjustment of those powers he places in the Deity. But as we never see matter without the adjustment of those properties as well as the existence of them, this drives him at last to say, the Deity must also have created matter, according to his system eternally created it, cotemporarily with himself. Ideas absurd and irreconcileable!

Discoursing upon the hypothesis of "a fortuitous concourse of atoms" Dr. Priestley asks, "what reason we have to think that small masses of matter can have power without communication *ab extra*?" Let this question be returned, "have we not reason to think so from attraction the most common property in matter." To get rid of this difficulty he will not allow an atom of matter to be possessed originally of the most simple powers, though he is ready to allow matter to have been eternal. A magnet according to this system must sometime have existed without its magnetic power. He concludes there must be some original existent Being. He shall be allowed many original existent Beings if it pleases him. A man may be an originally existent being, as well as any other. He is superior to other animals in this world. In like manner there may be allowed superior Beings to man (as most probably there are) and yet those superior Beings not have made man.

Dr. Priestley will have it, that all bodies are moved by external force. That does not seem quite necessary. Motion may as well be asserted to be originally a property of matter, or its true natural state and rest a deprivation of that property, as that rest should be its natural state. Hume thought so and Hume was no great fool, notwithstanding Dr. Priestley makes so light of him. In fact matter never is, and therefore most probably never was found to be in a state of rest. Nor has Dr. Priestley any reason to suppose gravity, elasticity and electricity to have been imprest on bodies by a superior Being, and not originally inherent in matter, unless to favour his own hypothesis of a Deity. He absolutely says matter could not have had those powers without a communication from a superior and intelligent Being. If matter is perceived in regulated motion, it is added bluntly, that it must be by a mover possessed of a competent intelligence, and that a Being therefore of such power and intelligence *must* exist. Whoever finds no difficulty in believing the contrary will find as little difficulty in Mr. Hume's hypothesis, that motion might as well as other powers and properties have been originally inherent in matter, or at least have been a necessary result of some matter acting upon another.

It has always been a doubt with Theists, whether they can better prove their God's existence by moral or physical considerations. Dr. Priestley seems to think the *forte* of the argument lies in the latter proof, and lays particular stress upon his observation respecting cause and effect, which therefore cannot here be so readily dismissed. He makes great reference to the works of art. Theists are always for turning their God into an overgrown man. Anthropomorphites has long been a term applied to them. They give him hands and eyes nor can they conceive him otherwise than as a corporeal Being. In which, as before has been said, they are very right, for there can only be in the world body and the space which bodies occupy. But granting this great workman to have done so much, is it not quite an incontrovertible proposition, that whoever first made a thing, as, for example, a chair or a table, must have had an adequate idea of it's nature and use. Dr. Priestley speaks more correctly in another part, by saying, he must have been *capable* of comprehending it. The nature and use of things are often found out after they are made and by different persons than the makers of them. Neither is there any analogy between the works of art, as a table or house, and of nature, as a man or tree. Therefore there can be no arguing from one to another by analogy. Hume observes that the former works are done by reason and design, and the latter by generation and vegetation, and therefore arguing from effect to causes, it is probable, that the universe is generated or vegetated. At least after all the observations about a table, it may be modestly asked, whether there is not some difference between a table and the world? The Doctor will also find some difficulty in explaining the propriety of any argument of analogy between men and metals, which he does not at other times scruple to make?

A *gratis* assertion is first made, that all things we see are effects; then because we see one thing caused, every thing must have been caused. His conclusion of the argument is still more curious, "because every thing was caused there must have been something that was not caused." The cause ought to be proportioned to the effect. The effect is not infinite. Why then attribute infinity to the cause? This is Hume's argument. Priestley calls it shortly unworthy of a philosopher. Let others judge! But surely, with all this infinity it may be asked, why may not there have been an infinity of causes?

Another argument is, that being unable to account, for what is, by any thing visible, we must have recourse to something invisible, and that invisible power is what he calls God. Apply this argument to gravity, and the external force that is said to cause every stone to fall is God. But if nothing visible can to us account for the operations of nature, why must we have recourse to what is invisible? Why necessary to account at all for them? Or why may not visible things account for them, although this person or another cannot tell which?

If nothing can begin to exist of itself or by the energy of material nature, it is more consistent to allow a plurality of Deities, than one immediate Deity. An equality in a plurality of Deities might be objectionable. But that is not at all necessary, rather the contrary; and so was the Pagan theory, which is not so absurd as the modern one. This universe or mundane system may be the work of one hand, another of another, and so on. Where is the absurdity of that? If the universe is applied to the solar system, there is an appearance of its being formed by one design, and in that stile it might be said to be the work of one hand. But this Deity is asserted to be infinite, and to have made all other worlds and universes, though it does not appear by any unity of design that all other worlds and universes are one work with this.

Dr. Priestley himself allows that reason would drive us to require a cause of the Deity. He is himself obliged to conclude, after all his reasoning, that we must acquiesce in our inability of having any idea on the subject; that is, how God could exist without a prior cause. At the same time he says the Deity cannot have a cause, and therefore we cannot reason about him. Why then all his own reasoning? We make a Deity ourselves, fall down and worship him. It is the molten calf over again. Idolatry is still practised. The only difference is that now we worship idols of our imagination; before of our hands. "Still we must necessarily rest at a Being that is infinite;" that is, when our reason drives us to the admission of an infinite cause we must necessarily stop finitely in our career. Not content with this conclusion he adds, that we cannot help perceiving the existence of this cause, though he owns that it is not an object of our conceptions. But even the Theist's argument does not necessarily drive us to the admission of an infinite cause. The argument is, "because there is a man, and man has intelligence, we must necessarily admit of a Being of infinitely superior intelligence." Would it not be nearly as well to argue, "because there is a goose, therefore there must be a man."

What is there more which hinders a series of finite causes to be carried back *ad infinitum*, than that the reasoner or contemplator of the course of nature is tired. If this eternal series could not exist, a Deity might with some propriety be said to follow. Put the argument into a syslogistic form.

"The universe shews design;"

"It is absurd to suppose an infinite succession of finite causes;"

"Therefore there is an uncaused intelligent cause of this universe."

Deny the second assertion and the problem is destroyed. So far from its being difficult to suppose an eternity, it is the most difficult thing in the world to suppose any thing but an eternity. A mind, not afraid to think, will find it the most easy contemplation in the world to dwell upon. It is at least a bold assertion, that *nothing can be more evident* than that plants and animals could not have proceeded from each other by succession from all eternity. Surely to this may be answered, that it is more evident that two and two make four. But Dr. Priestley goes on to say, "that the primary cause of a man cannot be a man, any more than the cause of a sound can be a sound." Experience shews us all sound is an effect of a cause. Does experience shew us more of a man than that he came from a man and a woman? To allow therefore that all men must have come from a man and a woman is as far as we can argue upon the subject, whilst in reasoning we trust to experience. An argument is well built upon similarity, therefore it is probable if one horse had a cause all horses had. But will not the argument be more consonant to itself, in supposing all horses had the same cause, and as one is seen to be generated from a horse and a mare so all were from all eternity. It were a better argument in favour of a Deity or some invisible agent to shew that a new animal came every now and then into life, without any body's knowing how or where.

It is allowed by Priestley and all other reasoners, that the most capital argument that can be formed in support of any thesis is to be built upon experience, or analogy to experience. Yet will many of these reasoners, Dr. Priestley at least for one, contend at the same time for the probability of a future life, when no instance can be given of any revival whatsoever. The same will contend, that their Deity can at pleasure form new species of animals, though in fact we never do see new beings come into existence. We ought only to argue from experience; and experience would teach us, that the species of all animals has eternally existed. Grant that we do not know, whether man has been eternal, or from a time, is it therefore because we do not know, that we must say he came from God? That unknown Being, as he is sometimes pompously and ridiculously called! The Devil is equally an unknown Being. The admission of evil under a good Deity opens a ready door to the manichean system, which seems much more rational than simple Deism.

The following chain of reasoning, as used by Dr. Priestley, is well linked together to prove the weight and force of experience in reasoning, but it proves nothing more. "Chairs and tables are made by men or beings of similar powers, because we see them made by men; and we cannot suppose them made by a tree or come into being of themselves, because that is against experience. No one will say one table might make another, or that one man might make another. We see nothing come into being without an adequate cause." Yet for this adequate cause we are at the same time referred to a belief in a causeless secret invisible agent, and to our own experience, for a proof of his nature.

Dr. Priestley allows, that what is *visible* in man may be the feat of all his powers, for it is (as he says,) a rule in philosophy not to multiply causes without necessity. But he affirms that what is *visible* in the universe cannot be the feat of intelligence. This is breaking the very rule of reasoning which he himself has chosen to adopt; and he gives no other reason for it, than because we do not see the universe think as we do man. Sensible of this dilemma, soon afterwards he inclines to allow principle of thought to the universe, for he adds, that if we allow it, yet the universe has so much the appearance of other works of design that we must look out for its author as much as that of a man; and it is allowed that most probably it had the same author.

Every difficulty vanishes with the energy of nature, or at least is as well accounted for as from an independent Deity. It is an usual question to those philosophers, who maintain that the present existence of things is the result of the force and energy of nature acting upon herself, "why this force does not perpetually operate and produce new appearances?" Besides that this question may be retorted upon the supporters of a Deity, I am thoroughly persuaded, that this force is constantly in action, and that every change which animals and vegetables undergo, whether of dissolution or renovation, is a manifest and undeniable proof of it. Man, and the other Beings which occupy this terrestrial globe, are evidently suited to its present state, and an alteration in their habitation, such as that of extreme or excessive heat, would inevitably destroy them. This is so certain, that bones of animals have been dug up which appertain to no species now existing, and which must have perished from an alteration in the system of things taking place too considerable for it to endure. Whenever the globe shall come to that temperament fit for the life of that lost species, whatever energy in nature produced it originally, if even it had a beginning, will most probably be sufficient to produce it again. Is not the reparation of vegitable life the spring equally wonderful now as its first production? Yet this is a plain effect of the influence of the sun, whose absence would occasion death by a perpetual winter. So far this question from containing, in my opinion, a formidable difficulty to the Epicurean system, I cannot help judging the continual mutability of things as an irrefragable proof of this eternal energy of nature. Those who ask, why the great changes in the state of things are not more frequent, would absurdly require them to ensue within the short space of their existence, forgetting that millions of ages are of no importance to the whole mass of matter, though Beings of some particular forms may find a wish and an advantage to prolong the term of their duration under that form.

If it is said, Nature or the energy of nature is another name for the Deity, then may Dr. Priestley and his answerer shake hands; the one is no more an atheist than the other. And if it is observed that the Energy of Nature having produced men may be capable of re-producing them, so that an atheist is not sure to escape punishment for his crimes, it is easy to say in return, neither is a Deist sure. A good atheist has no more reason to be afraid to be re-produced than a good Deist or a Christian. It may be useful for both of them to be good. If necessary let it again be repeated, that it is not at all meant in this answer to make atheism a plea or protection for immorality. That is a charge long and most unjustly put upon the poor undefended atheist. The knowledge of a God and even the belief of a providence are found but too slight a barrier against human passions, which are apt to fly out as licentiously as they would otherwise have done. All, which this creed can in reality produce, scarce goes beyond some exterior exercises, which are vainly thought to reconcile man to God. It may make men build temples, sacrifice victims, offer up prayers, or perform something of the like nature; but never break a criminal intrigue, restore an ill gotten wealth, or mortify the lust of man. Lust being the source of every crime, it is evident (since it reigns as much among idolaters and anthropomorphites, as among atheists) idolaters and anthropomorphites must be as susceptible of all of crimes as atheists, and neither the one set nor the other could form societies, did not a curb, stronger then that of religion, namely human laws, repress their perverseness. If no other remedy were applied to vice than the remonstrances of divines, a great city such as London, would in a fortnight's time, fall into the most horrid disorders. Whatever may be the difference of faith, vice predominates alike with the Christian and the Jew, with the Deist and the atheist. So like are they in their actions, that one would think they copied one another. Religion may make men follow ceremonies; little is the inconvenience found in them. A great triumph truly for religion to make men baptise or fast? When did it make men do virtuous actions for virtue's sake, or practise fewer inventions to get rich, where riches could not be acquired without poverty to others? The true principle most commonly seen in human actions, and which philosophy will cure sooner than religion, is the natural inclination of man for pleasure, or a taste contracted for certain objects by prejudice and habit. These prevail in whatsoever faith a man is educated, or with whatever knowledge he may store his mind.

But it will be said, those who commit crimes are atheists at the time at least they do so. But an atheist cannot be superstitious, and criminals are often so at the very moment of their crimes. Religious persuasion men are not doubted to have when they vent their rage upon others of a different way of thinking, when they express a dread of danger or a zeal for ceremonies. These at least are not virtues; and few indeed must be those, who at any time are really Theists, if their faith is lost or forgotten every time they have a mind to indulge a vitious passion. To support still the efficacy of religion in making men virtuous is to oppose metaphysical reasoning to the truth of fact; it is like the philosopher denying motion, and being refuted by one of his scholars walking across the room. If then it is true, as history and the whole course of human life shew it is, that men can still plunge themselves into all sorts of crimes, though they are persuaded of the truth of religion, which is made to inform them that God punishes sin and rewards good actions, it cannot but be suspected that religion even encourages crimes, by the hopes it gives of pardon through the efficacy of prayer; at all events it must be granted, that those who hold up a belief in God as a sufficient proof and character of a good life are most egregiously mistaken.

Some Theists may have lighter sense of personal dignity than some atheists. If the Theist thinks himself allied to and connected with the Deity he may plume himself upon his station; but how apt are those worshipers of a God, instead of having a high sense of personal dignity, to debase themselves into the most abject beings, dreading even the shadow of their own phantom. An atheist feeling himself to be a link in the grand chain of Nature, feels his relative importance and dreads no imaginary Being. An atheist, who is so from inattention and without intelligence, may indeed feel himself as much debased as the meanest and most humble Theist.

Another argument against atheists is, that where men are atheists it is generally found that their usual turn of thinking and habits of life have inclined to make them so. Is not this to be turned upon Theists? But granting that the idea of a supreme author is more pleasing, and that the argument with respect to the existence or non-existence of a God was in *equilibrio*, it is not therefore right to conclude that the mind ought to be determined by this or any other bias. Nor is it quite clear if there is no God (by which term let it again be noticed, is meant a Being of supreme intelligence, the contriver of the material universe and yet no part of the material system) that the world in which man inhabits is either fatherless or deserted. The wisdom of nature supplies in reality what is only hoped for from the protection of the Deity. If the world has so good a mother, a father may well be spared especially such a haughty jealous, and vindictive one as God is most generally represented to be. Dr. Priestley being clear in his opinion; that the being of a God is capable of being proved by reason, is not so weak as some of his fellow-labourers, who hold the powers of reason in so low estimation as to be incapable of themselves to arrive at almost any truth. He must however allow, if reason proves a Deity and his attributes there was less use of revelation to prove them. But the learned advocates of a Deity differ greatly among themselves, whether his existence is capable of being ascertained by fixt principles of reason. After such a difference and the instance of so many great men in all ages, from Democritus downward, who have confidently denied the being of a God, whose arguments the learned Dr. Cudworth, in the last century, only by fully and fairly stating, with all the answers in his power to give (though his zeal in religion was never doubted) was thought by other divines to have given a weight to atheism not well to be overturned, it is surprising that it should be the common belief of this day, that an argument in support of atheism cannot stand a moment, and that even no man in his senses can ever hold such a doctrine. All that Epicurus and Lucretius have so greatly and convincingly said is swept away in a moment by these better reasoners, who yet scruple not to declare, with Dr. Priestley, that what they reason about is not the subject of human understanding. But let it be asked, is it not absurd to reason with a man about that of which that same man asserts we have no idea at all? Yet will Dr. Priestley argue, and say it is of no importance, whether the person with whom he argues has a conception or not of the subject. "Having no ideas includes no impossibility," therefore he goes on with his career of words to argue about an unseen being with another whom he will allow to have no idea of the subject and yet it shall be of no avail in the dispute, whether he has or no, or whether he is capable or incapable of having any. Reason failing, the passions are called upon, and the imagined God is represented at one time, with all the terrors of a revengeful tyrant, at another with all the tenderness of an affectionate parent. Shall then such a tremendous Being with such a care for the creatures he has made, suffer his own existence to be a perpetual doubt? If the course of nature does not give sufficient proof, why does not the hand divine shew itself by an extraordinary interposition of power? It is allowed miracles ought not to be cheap or plenty. One or two at least every thousand years might be admitted. But this is a perpetual standing miracle, that such a Being as the depicted God, the author of nature and all its works, should exist and yet his existence be perpetually in doubt, or require a Jesus, a Mahomet or a Priestley to reveal it. Is not the writing of this very answer to the last of those three great luminaries of religion a proof, that no God, or no *such* God at least, exists. Hear the admirable words of the author of "The System of Nature;" *Comment permet il qu'un mortel comme moi ose attaquer ses droits, ses titres, son existence meme?*

Dr. Clarke, Mr. Hume and Helvetius, are writers whose arguments for and against a Godhead Dr. Priestley has much noted. The former says, "the Deity must have been infinite, if self-existent, because all things in the universe are made by him." Are all things in the universe infinite? Why an infinite maker of a finite work? It is juster to argue, that whatever is self-existent must have been eternal. Nor is there any great objection to the converse of the proposition properly taken, that whatever is not self-existent must have been created and therefore cannot have been eternal. If this is fair arguing, matter cannot according to Dr. Priestley's system have been created and be eternal also. But Dr. Priestley has no inclination to reconcile his opinions with those of Dr. Clarke. He has chosen a fairer method, and that is, to refute the arguments of former asserters of a Deity as well as to establish his own. Dr. Clarke he most effectually exposes where he enters upon the subject of space. It seems as if Dr. Clarke, having asserted that the Deity necessarily existed, had a mind that nothing else should necessarily exist but the Deity; and conscious that space at least also necessarily existed, he makes universal space an attribute of the Deity. With this reverie in his head he raises a syllogism of complete nonsense (*vide Priestley's Letters*, P. 170.) where he supposes space to be nothing though he also supposes it to be an attribute of the Deity. Making it therefore an attribute of the Deity and knowing that space is eternal and unmeasurable he takes upon himself thereby also clearly to have proved that the Deity is so. Exclude the Deity, space will still exist and still be eternal and immense. Dr. Priestley knew well that Dr. Clarke's argument in this respect was all a fallacy, and therefore he shews his sense in not adopting it. It is in fact an abuse of terms unworthy of a scientific reasoner.

The only argument attempted by Dr. Clarke, why the Deity must have had no cause, is, because it is necessary he should have none. Dr. Clarke says roundly that necessity is the cause of the existence of the Deity. This is very near the language of the ancients, who held that Fate controuled the Gods. Necessity is therefore the first God. Why then any other God than Necessity? What more has Helvetius said than that?

It is an old and unanswerable argument that, granting a God and his power infinite, whatever he wills is executed; but man and other animals are unhappy, therefore he does not will they should be happy. Or take the argument the other way and it will equally conclude against his power. With regard to Mr. Hume's famous observations upon the evidence of miracles, Dr. Priestley thinks to make a short havock of them by observing that new, and therefore miraculous appearances, are continually presenting themselves; but although such new appearances may be instanced, they are not contrary to former experience, only in addition to it. With this allusion to Natural Philosophy, Dr. Priestley thinks himself in one short sentence to have discussed all Mr. Hume's observations upon miracles. *"Which is more likely, that the relater of a miracle should have lied or been deceived, or that the thing related should have existed contrary to experience prior and subsequent?"* Let the force of this observation be considered and believe in the history of miracles who can! To give a finishing stroke to poor Mr. Hume, Dr. Priestley observes that literary fame was Hume's only motive and consolation, as he said himself, in all his laborious enquiries and enlightened writings. At this he exclaims, "What gloomy prospect and poor comfort he must have had at his death!" If so, how much was he the greater man so well to have gone through that last scene!

The honour which Dr. Priestley gives to Helvetius, the author of that ingenious and satisfactory work intitled "The System of Nature," does credit to his own candour. He applauds him for speaking out, he ought therefore to applaud this answer for the same reason. It is true he seems to have discovered one incongruity in the reasoning of Helvetius. The words he imputes to him are, "that nature has no object, because nature acts necessarily; man has an object; yet man also acts necessarily." In the same way nature might have an object though it acted necessarily. But Helvetius adds, that the object which man has is a necessary object. The best defence of Helvetius (not in behalf of that passage, but of his general system) is to let him speak at large for himself; and the following quotation Dr. Priestley and the reader may accept as a specimen of the strength and justice of his argument, and as the conclusion of this answer.

"Theologians tell us, that the disorder and evil, which is seen in the world, is not absolute and real, but relatively and apparently such, and does not disprove the divine wisdom and goodness. But may not one reply, that the goodness and wonderful order which they so much extol, and on which they found their notions of those qualities in God, are in a similar way only relative and apparent. If it be only our co-existence with the causes which surround us, and our manner of perceiving them, that constitute the order of nature for us, and authorise us to attribute wisdom and goodness to the maker of what surround us, should not also our mode of existence and perception authorise us to call what is hurtful to us disorder, and to attribute impotence, ignorance, or malice, to that Being which we would suppose to actuate nature.

Some pretend that the supremely wise God can derive goodness and happiness to us from the midst of those ills which he permits us to undergo in this world. Are these men privy counsellors of the Divinity, or on what do they found their romantic hopes? They will doubtless say, that they judge of God's conduct by analogy, and that from the present appearance of his wisdom and goodness, they have a right to infer his future wisdom and goodness. But do not the present appearances of his want of wisdom or goodness justify us in concluding, that he will always want them? If they are so often manifestly deficient in this world, what can assure us that they will abound more in the next? This kind of language therefore rests upon no other basis than a prejudiced imagination, and signifies, that some men, having without examination, adopted an opinion that God is good, cannot admit that he will consent to let his creatures remain constantly unhappy. Yet this grand hypothesis, of the unalterable felicity of mankind hereafter, is insufficient to justify the Divinity in permitting the present sleeting and transitory marks of injustice and disorder. If God can have been unjust for a moment, he has derogated, during that moment at least, from his divine perfection, and is not unchangeably good; his justice then is liable to temporary alteration, and, if this be the case, who can give security for his justice and goodness continuing unalterable in a future life, the notion of which is set up only to exculpate his deviation from those qualities in this?

In spite of the experience, which every instant gives the lie to that beneficence which men suppose in God, they continue to call him good. When we bewail the miserable victims of those disorders and calamities that so often overwhelm our species, we are confidently told that these ills are but apparent, and that if our short-sighted mind could fathom the depths of divine wisdom, we should always behold the greatest blessings result from what we denominate evil. How despicable is so frivolous an answer! If we can find no good but in such things as affect us in a manner which is agreeable and pleasing to our actual existence, we shall be obliged to confess that those things which affect us, even but for a time, in, a painful manner, are as certainly evil to us. To vindicate God's visiting mankind with these evils some tell us, that he is just, and that they, are chastisements inflicted on mankind to punish the wrongs he has received from men. Thus a feeble mortal has the power to irritate and injure the almighty and eternal Being who created this world. To offend any one is, to afflict him, to diminish in some degree his happiness, to make him feel a painful sensation. How can man possibly disturb the felicity of the all-powerful sovereign of nature! How can a frail creature, who has received from God his being and his temper, act against the inclinations of an irresistable force which never consents to sin and disorder? Besides justice, according to the only ideas which we can have of it, supposes a fixt desire to render every one his due. But theologians constantly preach that God owes us nothing, that the good things he affords are the voluntary effects of his beneficence, and that without any violence of his equity he can dispose of his creatures as his choice or caprice may impel him. In this doctrine I see not the smallest shadow of justice, but the most hideous tyranny and shocking abuse of power. In fact do we not see virtue and innocence plunged into an abyss of misery, while wickedness rears its triumphant head under the empire of this God whose justice is so much extalled? "This misery, say you, is but for a time." Very well, Sirs, but your God is unjust for a time. "He chastises whom he loves (you will say) for their own benefit." But if he is perfectly good, why will he let them suffer at all? "He does it, perhaps to try them" But, if he knows all things, what occasion is there for him to try any? If he is omnipotent, why need he vex himself about the vain design any one may form against him? Omnipotence ought to be exempt from any such passions, as having neither equals nor rivals. But if this God is jealous of his glory, his titles and prerogative, why does he permit such numbers of men to offend him? Why are any found daring enough to refuse the incense which his pride expects? *Why am I a feeble mortal permitted to attack his titles, his attributes, and even his existence?* Is this permission of punishment on me for the abuse of his grace and favour? He should never have permitted me to abuse them. Or the grace he bestowed should have been efficacious and have directed my steps according to his liking. "But, say you, he makes man free." Alas? why did he present him with a gift of which he must have foreseen the abuse? Is this faculty of free agency, which enables me to resist his power, to corrupt and rob him of his worshippers, and in fine to bring eternal misery on myself, a present worthy of his infinite goodness? In consequence of the pretended abuse of this fatal present, which an omniscient and good God ought not to have bestowed on Beings capable of abusing it, everlasting, inexpressible torments are reserved for the transitory crimes of a Being made liable to commit them. Would that father be called good, reasonable, just and kind, who put a sharp-edged and dangerous knife into the hand of a playful, and imprudent child, whom he before knew to be imprudent, and punished him during the remainder of his life for cutting himself with it? Would that prince be called just and merciful, who, not regarding any proportion between the offence and the punishment, should perpetually exercise his power of vengeance, over one of his subjects who, being drunk, had rashly offended against his vanity, without causing any real harm to him, especially, when the prince had taken pains to make him drunk? Should we consider as almighty a monarch, whose dominions were in such confusion and disorder, that, except a small number obedient servants, all his subjects were every instant despising his laws, defeating his will and insulting his person? Let ecclesiastics then acknowledge, that their God is an assemblage of incompatible qualities, as incomprehensible to their understanding as to mine. No: they say, in reply to these difficulties, that wisdom and justice in God, are qualities so much above or so unlike those qualities in us, that they bear no relation or affinity towards human wisdom and justice. But, pray how am I to form to myself an idea of the divine perfection, unless it has some resemblance to those virtues which I observe in my fellow creatures and feel in myself? If the justice of God is not the same with human justice, why lastly do any men pretend to announce it, comprehend and explain it to others?"

POSTSCRIPT.

Previous to this publication the editor sent the following Letter to Dr. Priestley.

"Reverend Sir,

Had you thought it impossible for man to hold different sentiments respecting Natural religion and the proof of the existence of a God than you do, the Letters to a Philosophical Unbeliever would not have appeared, much less would you have invited an answer by promising a reply to every objection. Differing from you in sentiment I am the man who enter with you in the lists; but I find myself upon consultation with my friends under more difficulties than you were, and more to stand in need of courage in taking up the glove, than you needed to have in throwing it down. For this dispute is not like others in philosophy, where the vanquished can only dread ridicule, contempt and disappointment; here, whether victor or vanquished, your opponent has to dread, beside ecclesiastical censure, the scourges, chains and pillories of the courts of Law.

I accuse you not of laying a trap for an unguarded author, but I ask your friendly opinion, whether I can, with temporal safety at least, maintain the contrary of your arguments in proof of a Deity and his attributes. If I cannot, no wonder the Theist cries *Victoria!* but then it is a little ungenerous to ask for objections. Of you, I may certainly expect, that you will promise to use your influence, as well with lawyers as ecclesiastics, not to stir up a persecution against a poor atheist in case there should be one found in the kingdom, which people in general will not admit to be possible; or, if a persecution could ensue, that you and your friends, favourers of free enquiry, will at least bear the expences of it.

I am,
Reverend Sir,
Your most humble obedient servant,
WILLIAM HAMMON.

Oct. 23. 1781.

To the Reverend Dr. Priestley.

To this letter Dr. Priestley sent no answer; or no answer ever came to hand.

THE END.

Lector House believes that a society develops through a two-fold approach of continuous learning and adaptation, which is derived from the study of classic literary works spread across the historic timeline of literature records. Therefore, we aim at reviving, repairing and redeveloping all those inaccessible or damaged but historically as well as culturally important literature across subjects so that the future generations may have an opportunity to study and learn from past works to embark upon a journey of creating a better future.

This book is a result of an effort made by Lector House towards making a contribution to the preservation and repair of original ancient works which might hold historical significance to the approach of continuous learning across subjects.

HAPPY READING & LEARNING!

LECTOR HOUSE LLP
E-MAIL: lectorpublishing@gmail.com